Easy Chinese Cookbook

77 Quick and Easy Dishes to Prepare at Home
veggie dishes

By

Jerry C. Mabry

Table of contents

Introduction

A significant part of Chinese food in Chinese culture comprises of cuisines from different areas of China and overseas Chinese who have lived in other regions of the world. Due to the Chinese immigrant community and its historical strength, many other foods in Asia have been inspired by Chinese cuisine with changes made to appeal to local features. The ingredients used in Chinese cuisine are available worldwide as essential components of Chinese food such as soy sauce, noodles, rice, chili oil, tea, tofu, and cookware such as wok and chopsticks.

Chinese regions' tastes for spice and preparation techniques rely on variations in historical background and people migrated from different regions. Geographical location, including cliffs, rivers, trees, and plains, also significantly impact the locally available components, noting that the weather of China ranges from tropical climates to subarctic in the northeast. The taste and presentation of the food is enhanced through the use of proper instruments, accurate cooking time, and calculated measurement of the spices.

Special veggies used in Chinese food include bok choy, snow peas, baby corn, Chinese broccoli, Chinese eggplant, and straw mushrooms. Other veggies are often used in China's various cuisines, namely pea vine tops, watercress, water chestnuts, bean sprouts, chestnuts, lotus roots, and bamboo shoots. Cultivars of peas, green beans, and mushrooms can be recognized in a wide variety owing to varying climatic and soil factors. Several dry or salted veggies are also produced, particularly in drier or cooler areas where it is difficult to get fresh produce out of season.

Vegetarian dishes are widespread and freely accessible in China, but only a smaller proportion of the population practices veganism. A focus on fresh veggies, especially in rural areas, renders Chinese food perfect for vegans. The foundations of Chinese food, noodles, rice, and herbs are all perfect for vegans. "Vegetarian Chinese Cookbook" has all vegetarian recipes. It has four chapters with a short introduction to Chinese cuisine and some historical facts. Chapter two, three, and four discuss Chinese breakfasts, snacks, lunch, dinner, soups, and a few famous vegetarian recipes from Chinese cuisine. Learn 77 recipes of delicious and easy Chinese vegetarian cuisine from this book and prepare your vegan meals.

Chapter 1: A Brief Introduction to Chinese Food

Chinese food (Chinese meals) developed in the various areas of China has been popular in many other places of the globe. Within China's different areas, local cultural variations differ tremendously. Considering the significance of rice in the Chinese food in daily meals, no rice is often provided at all on highly formal events. In such a situation, rice will be offered only if no other dishes exist, or as a consolation dish in the type of sticky rice at the end of dinner. Soup is commonly eaten at the beginning of food as a side dish and at the end of dinner.

In Chinese tradition, chopsticks are the main feeding utensil for food, whereas soups and other fluids are eaten with a long, plain spoon. In the history, costlier items were used including silver and ivory. On the other side, plastic chopsticks crafted of bamboo/wood have mostly substituted disposable ones in chain shops.

Food is served in bite-sized parts (for example, vegetables, beef, and tofu) in most Chinese food recipes, ready for immediate filling up and consumption. Since these devices are seen as weapons, Chinese society has been utilizing forks and knives at the Iron plate barbaric. It is often deemed impolite to make visitors split their food by operating on it.

Fish are typically fried and eaten in uncut form, unlike the other food where they are initially sliced open, and chefs directly take bits from the salmon with tools to consume. It is because it is desirable to serve seafood as clean as necessary. The vegetarian diet in China is not rare or exceptional. However, it is still followed by a comparatively limited percentage of the population, and the same situation is there in the West. Unlike the traditional perception of the West, Chinese vegan diets are not cooked in lots of oils.

1.1 History and Facts of Chinese Food

China has a history of being the Culinary Empire. The diverse geographical climate, local goods and materials, local rituals, cultural practices, ethnic roots, and some of the common tasty cultural varieties have played a major role in the growth of Chinese food as it is nowadays. Chinese food can differentiate the various tastes between the Northern and Southern foods during the East Zhou period. During Song and Tang Dynasties, South food and North food's feature starts to build, and it continues to grow until the earliest Qing dynasty. By the period of later Confucius and Zhao, the Chinese Cuisine skills had achieved some levels. The theory of eating was debated and evaluated solely on aroma, flavor, texture, and shape. The Four Nature-hot, humid, cold, and cool, along with the Five Flavor, sweet, salty, sour, bitter, and acidic, complement a good meal. With local adaptation to appeal to the local palate, Chinese food has an impact over most of the other foods, especially in the Asian region.

Chinese food is seldom considered to be just food; for the Chinese people, it has a combination of literature, ideology, and profound cultural definitions. With decades of tradition, the knowledge of Chinese cuisine is sure to amaze and impress everyone. Sometimes, visitors are surprised by what the Chinese are eating. But modernist cuisine in numerous restaurants worldwide often encompasses a variety of safe, clean, and mindful food. There are more than a hundred ways to prepare food, with explicit amounts of nutritious vegetables and delicious ingredients. Rice, pasta, barley, soybeans, beans, vegetables, spices, and flavorings are the essential foods and additives used in the Chinese cuisine. It was not just because of the large scale of Chinese territory, but because their cuisine was highly valued by their rulers and chefs, that is why Chinese foods got popular in the world. Curries, Chinese coleslaw, sausage rolls, tofu goods, snack, and frozen dishes are the most common food forms in China.

1.2 Chinese Cuisine- Cooking Methods

Chinese cuisine is popular all over the world. Chinese cuisine has its unique cooking style. In terms of color, form, and appearance, the attention is on clean, seasonal products, cooked with a minimal hassle and finely presented food.

Deep-Fry

For providing buttery texture to dishes, deep-frying is being used. It is typically used in the oil warmed to extreme temperatures to cook a range of vegetables and meat. Deep frying is achieved using a large deep fryer or saucepan, a Chinese scrape sieve, and large chopsticks.

Stir-Fry

The traditional Chinese method of preparing is stir-frying. Stir-frying is simple, fast, delicious and tasty. The preparation utensils include a spoon for the wok and skillet. Stir-frying is usually carried out on a stovetop, but an electric stove may be used if heated up to a high temperature. Usually, stir-frying is used to cook a combination of fish or meat, onions, and tofu. Every product is cut or roughly chopped. Using salt, soy sauce, and other spices, the meat or fish is marinated.

Steam

Steaming is a cooking process that uses steam. It is deemed a healthful method for cooking. Steaming process makes meals more flavorful and clean. It can maintain different nutrients in the diet and, to a large degree, it can reduce the nutritional loss. Dishes that need the highest temperature during preparation are placed next to the hot water on the bottom side, while those that need less temperature are positioned on the upper layer. The water must be maintained at a steady boil until the cooking is finished.

Braising

Braising means adding vegetables, herbs, spices, and a small volume of water or liquid in a saucepan or wok and briefly heating it together at extreme temperatures, and afterward simmering this for a long period at a reduced speed. The products are normally sliced into crystals or huge cubes. All of the meal is prepared properly using this method.

Roasting

It is possible to cook many Chinese meals like a duck, chicken, the whole cow, a whole pig, and a sheep's leg with this cooking method. Meat is generally prepared and either hung over a flame or put in a really hot oven. For the skin to appear juicy, the meat must be pickled. It is then sliced until the meat has been grilled, skillfully placed on a pan, and eaten with a creamy sauce from meat cooking liquid. Peking duck is among the most popular roasted recipes.

Chapter 2: Vegetarian Chinese Lunch and Dinner

2.1 Vegetarian Lunch Recipes

Vegetable Fried Rice

Cooking Time: 45 minutes

Serving Size: 4

Ingredients:

- ⅛ teaspoon white pepper
- 1 tablespoon Shaoxing wine
- 2 tablespoons vegetable oil
- 1 clove garlic (minced)
- 1 scallion (chopped)
- 2 cups mung bean sprouts
- 4 ½ cups cooked white rice
- ¼ cup bell pepper
- ¾ cup snow peas (chopped)
- ¼ cup carrots (diced)
- ¼ cup fresh shiitake mushrooms (diced)
- ½ teaspoon sesame oil
- ½ teaspoon turmeric
- ½ cup onion (diced)
- 2 teaspoons light soy sauce
- ½ teaspoon salt

- 2 teaspoons dark soy sauce

For the Eggs

- ½ teaspoon Shaoxing wine
- 2 tablespoons vegetable oil
- ¼ teaspoon salt
- ⅛ teaspoon white pepper
- 2 eggs

Method:

1. Clean, drain, and steam your rice, and cook it as you usually do, whether in your crockpot or by using the roasting rack rice cooking process.

2. Add soy sauce, sesame oil, dark soy sauce, spice, turmeric to the rice and vegetables.

3. Mix till the ingredients and grains are well-mixed. Get the rice fried.

4. Let it out to chill exposed for five minutes after the rice is prepared.

5. With chopsticks or a spoon, whip the rice and switch it onto a serving platter or sheets pan to cool more and partially dry out.

6. You must see single rice grains that are not too if you have cooked the rice correctly.

7. Dice and cut all of the veggies including green pepper, green beans, tomatoes, mushrooms, carrots, and scallions; make sure they are all around the same size.

8. The mung green beans are the exception, which only needs to be washed, dried, and cut. In tidy stacks, set the veggies back.

9. Combine the flour, Shaoxing wine, and white pepper with the shells. Beat up for thirty seconds.

10. Heat the skillet until it starts to flame, and apply two tablespoons of neutral oil.

11. Place the egg mixture in.

12. Scramble them, then turn the heat off until they are about half finished.

13. To split the eggs into tiny chunks, use the flat spatula to use the wok's remaining heat for cooking them through.

14. Set it aside from the skillet.

15. Steam the skillet and put two tablespoons of oil, garlic, onion, and carrots into the skillet over medium-high heat. For two minutes, stir-fry.

16. Insert the bell peppers and mushrooms and proceed to stir-fry for the next sixty seconds.

17. Turn up the heat to the extreme, then add the rice.

18. Start stir-frying instantly and scrape up the skillet's ingredients vigorously from the base to keep the rice from clinging.

19. If you are using day-old rice, you should pour the sauce uniformly over the rice after two minutes and mix it until the rice has an even hue.

20. Insert the white pepper and proceed to stir-fry the rice for the next second.

21. When it is warmed through, you will also see steam beginning to emerge from the rice.

22. Insert the beans and mix for thirty seconds.

23. Add eggs till the whites are mixed and combined again.

24. Round the border of the skillet, add the Shaoxing wine, and mix it in.

25. Eventually, insert green onion and bean sprouts. Stir-fry before the sprouts of the beans only start to crumble and eat.

Vegetarian Chow Mein

Cooking Time: 30 minutes

Serving Size: 4

Ingredients:

- Freshly cracked pepper
- Optional: toasted sesame seeds
- 1 tablespoon brown sugar
- ½ teaspoon sesame oil
- ½ tablespoon cornstarch
- 1 ½ tablespoon lite soy sauce
- 1 ½ tablespoon vegetarian oyster sauce
- 1/3 cup veggie stock
- 1 ½ tablespoon vegetable oil
- 1 package (6 ounces) Chow Mein noodles
- 3 cups green cabbage
- 1 ½ cups baby belle mushrooms
- ¼ cup green onions
- ½ tablespoon fresh ginger
- ¾ cup sliced celery
- 1 ½ cups red pepper
- ¾ cup julienned carrots
- ½ tablespoon fresh garlic

Method:

1. Arrange the ingredients. Tear the cabbage thinly, mince the garlic and ginger thinly sliced.

2. Slice the carrots and then mash them into really tiny bits. Cut the celery very finely.

3. Cut the red pepper finely and cut those small pieces in half if they are long.

4. Cut the mushrooms evenly. To separate the green root from the white, finely chop the spring onions.

5. You must get around ¼ cup of white stems, thinly cut. For afterward, save the finely diced green pieces.

6. In a small cup, insert the flour and soy sauces and stir using a spoon until absolutely smooth.

7. Mix in vegan brown sugar, oyster sauce, vegetarian stock, and sesame oil. Add seasonings according to taste.

8. Whisk when soft.

9. To cook the chow Mein pasta, follow box instructions.

10. In cold water, drain and set it aside. Warm vegetable oil over medium-high heat pan.

11. For a couple of minutes, insert the white parts of the onions and then the ginger and garlic.

12. Be very careful not to burn. Steam for about twenty seconds.

13. Add red peppers, carrots, and celery. Stir-fry, cooking for three minutes almost continually.

14. Insert in the mushrooms and cabbage that are sliced.

15. Keep stirring for the next 2-3 minutes before the vegetables are crunchy, and the cabbage is ripened. Mix in the mixtures and the fried noodles.

16. Flip for two minutes with tongs once caramelized, and spices are mixed.

17. Insert the spring onions and buttered sesame seeds into the finely diced tops if needed. Instantly serve.

Eggplant with Hot Garlic Sauce

Cooking Time: 20 minutes

Serving Size: 4

Ingredients:

- 1 tablespoon Chinese black vinegar
- ½ teaspoon sugar
- 1 green onion chopped
- 1 tablespoon soy sauce
- 2 tablespoons cooking oil
- 1 red Chile pepper
- ½ inch fresh ginger
- 2 cloves garlic
- 3 eggplant small

Method:

1. Add three tablespoons of the frying oil to a skillet or saucepan on medium temperature and stir to cover the skillet.

2. Add the eggplant in a thin layer when the skillet is warm.

3. Cook and turn over each part for two minutes, so they cook uniformly. Cook for another 2-3 minutes, sometimes tossing.

4. The texture of the eggplant should be brown, the surface rumpled and the flesh tender.

5. In the skillet, take out the eggplant and insert three tablespoons of cooking oil.

6. Add the garlic, red chili peppers, spring onions, and ginger.

7. Once they become citrusy, swirl these flavors.

8. Mix with the eggplant seasonings and stir fry for one moment.

9. To mix everything, add black vinegar, soy sauce, and sugar and mix. Instantly serve.

Chinese Vegetable Stir Fry

Cooking Time: 30 minutes

Serving Size: 4

Ingredients:

- 3 scallions, thinly sliced
- 1 tablespoon fresh ginger
- 1 red bell pepper
- 3 cloves garlic
- 1 pound broccoli
- 7 ounces shiitake mushrooms
- 1/3 cup soy sauce
- ¼ teaspoon dry mustard
- 2 tablespoons vegetable oil
- 1 tablespoon cornstarch
- ¼ teaspoon red pepper flakes
- 3 tablespoons water
- 1 teaspoon sesame oil
- 2 teaspoons sugar
- 2 tablespoons dry sherry

Method:

1. Mix the sesame seed, soy sauce, dried sherry, water, red pepper flakes, sugar, cornflour, and dried mustard in a shallow pan. Just put aside.

2. Bring 1-inch dry sherry to a fast boil in a large skillet over medium heat.

3. Insert the vegetables and steam once delicate, or three minutes.

4. To interrupt the food preparation, drain the broccoli in a saucepan and then run it under ice water. Put down and enable to drain entirely.

5. Wash dry in the pan. Transfer the vegetable oil to two tablespoons and cook over medium temperature.

6. Insert the red peppers and shiitake mushrooms and simmer until the mushrooms are golden brown and the peppers are tender, mixing periodically, for six minutes.

7. Add the garlic, green onions, and ginger; simmer for about thirty seconds, swirling continuously, until fragrant.

8. Transfer the broccoli to the skillet and stir for about two minutes until it is cooked up.

9. Add the sauce that was reserved. Toss and cook for about thirty seconds till the liquid is browned, and the veggies are uniformly covered.

10. Spray with deep green spring onions and pass to the serving bowl. If needed, serve with rice.

Spinach-Filled Won-Tons

Cooking Time: 40 minutes

Serving Size: 24

Ingredients:

- ½ teaspoon of pepper
- Pinch of salt
- Pinch of cayenne pepper
- ½ teaspoon of garlic powder
- 24 wonton wrapper
- Frozen spinach 12 oz.
- Olive oil
- 8 oz. Of low-fat cream cheese

Method:

1. Heat the oven to 375.

2. Combine all the ingredients, except for the wonton packets and oil, in a pan.

3. In the center of each wrap, put two teaspoons of the cheese mixture and flip the packet in half to make a triangular shape.

4. To seal the sides, brush your finger over the corners with just a little liquid.

5. Rub a little oil on top and put on a baking parchment lined baking sheet.

6. This makes around twenty wontons. Bake for fifteen minutes or until the wrappers are brown.

Tofu, Cashews and Vegetables Recipe

Cooking Time: 35 minutes

Serving Size: 4-6

Ingredients:

Sauce Ingredients

- 1 ½ teaspoons ginger
- 1 large garlic clove
- 2 tablespoons rice vinegar
- 1 tablespoon cornstarch
- ¼ cup soy sauce
- 3 tablespoons honey
- ¼ cup water

Cashew Tofu

- 1 cup roasted cashews

- toppings: green onions
- 1 large red bell peppers
- 1 small red onion
- 1 package tofu
- Black pepper
- 1 head broccoli
- 3 tablespoons olive oil
- Fine sea salt
- 1 tablespoon cornstarch

Method:

1. Put the tofu between two kitchen towels to soak moisture.

2. Then put a work surface on the front of the tofu, and place on the work surface a few large containers or pots or something you can comfortably balance.

3. Create a sauce for the stir-fry.

4. In the meantime, in a small pan, mix all of the components until mixed.

5. Cut the cube lengthened into ½-inch bricks until the tofu has been soaked, and slice the tofu into small bits.

6. Switch to a medium bowl only with tofu, sprinkled with one tablespoon of olive oil uniformly, and swirl until covered.

7. Stir over the tofu with the cornflour and a small pinch of pepper and salt, and mix until covered uniformly.

8. Heat one tablespoon of oil in a non-stick pan over moderate to low heat.

9. Add around a quarter of the tofu and sauté for about five minutes, turning halfway across, if both sides are fluffy and translucent.

10. Move the tofu and proceed with the leftover tofu on a different tray.

11. In a saucepan, insert the leftover oil and add the pepper, broccoli, and red onion.

12. To the sauté pot, transfer the nuts, stir-fry liquid, prepared tofu, and mix to blend.

13. Keep cooking for another two minutes before the sauce thickens.

14. Lift the pan from the flame and offer the stir-fry hot, coated with your preferred sauces, over pasta, rice, or quinoa.

Chinese Vegetables with Baby Corn

Cooking Time: 30 minutes

Serving Size: 4

Ingredients:

- Ginger 10 g, grated
- Sesame oil ½ teaspoon
- Vegetable oil 30 ml
- Garlic 1 clove, crushed
- Red peppers
- Clear honey 18 g
- Vegetable stock 60 ml
- Baby sweetcorn
- Soy sauce 30 ml
- Rice wine 30 ml
- Snow peas

- Scallion
- Broccoli
- Bok choy

Method:

1. Remove the seeds from the spices and thickly slice them. Slice the bok choy into thick strips. Cut the broccoli into strips.

2. Place the wine, soy sauce, honey, and the product around. Just put aside.

3. In a skillet or big clear deep fryer, add the oil.

4. Insert the harder veggies and cook for thirty seconds over a medium temperature.

5. Add the sugar, cover the pot for two minutes on medium heat.

6. With the ginger and garlic, add the faster boiling veggies and stir-fry for two minutes, till almost ready.

7. Mix in the baby bok choy and cook for two minutes till the veggies are all baked.

8. Put in the combination of soy sauce, stir-fry, and spray with sesame oil for two minutes.

2.2 Vegetarian Dinner Recipes

Vegan Chinese Kung Pao Tofu

Cooking Time: 60 minutes

Serving Size: 3

Ingredients:

- 1 pound firm or extra firm tofu

For the Marinade

- 2 tablespoons soy sauce
- 1 tablespoon sesame oil
- 1 tablespoon lime juice
- 3 tablespoons vegetable broth

For Stir-Frying

- 1 teaspoon hot sauce
- Salt and pepper to taste
- ½ small purple cabbage (sliced thinly)
- 1 tablespoon fresh parsley
- 2 tablespoons sesame oil
- ¼ cup vegetable broth
- ½ cup snow peas
- 1 tablespoon minced fresh ginger
- 1 small bok choy (chopped)
- 1 medium onion (diced)
- ¼ teaspoon red pepper flakes

- ½ cup sliced mushrooms
- 1 red bell pepper (diced)

Method:

1. Assemble the products for the tofu and seasoning.
2. Create a sauce: In a cup, add the broth of vegetables, lemon juice, sesame oil, and soy sauce.
3. Insert the tofu and enable it to sit for at least thirty minutes, stirring to cover the tofu well periodically.
4. Heat the oven to 375 F. Cover a baking tray with aluminum foil.
5. For fifteen minutes, bake the tofu, rotating once. Put aside.
6. Take the leftover ingredients.
7. Warm the sesame oil in a large frying pan or a skillet over moderate flame.
8. Insert the onions, green pepper, pieces of red pepper, mushroom, and herbs and sauté for five minutes, stirring regularly.
9. Transfer bok choy and vegetable broth and simmer for another five minutes.
10. Insert the green beans and vegetables.
11. Turn down the heat to a low level and add the leftover ingredients and tofu.
12. Heat until mixed and thoroughly cooked.

Veg Manchurian Recipe

Cooking Time: 45 minutes

Serving Size: 2

Ingredients:

For Vegetable Balls

- 1 teaspoon soy sauce
- 1 tablespoon water
- 2 teaspoon salt
- 3 tablespoon cornflour
- 2 tablespoons all-purpose flour
- 2 teaspoons black pepper
- 1 teaspoon ginger
- 1 teaspoon garlic
- ½ cup capsicum
- ½ cup spring onion
- ½ cup carrot
- ½ cup cabbage

For Manchurian Sauce

- 3 tablespoon cornflour
- 1 cup water
- Oil
- 1 ½ tablespoon salt
- 1 tablespoon black pepper
- 2 tablespoon garlic
- 1 teaspoon soya sauce
- 1 teaspoon vinegar
- 1 tablespoon ginger
- 2 tablespoon tomato ketchup
- 2 tablespoon chili sauce

- 2 tablespoon spring onion
- 1 teaspoon green chili

Method:

1. In a pan, mix garlic, ginger, cornstarch, all-purpose flour, cinnamon, soy sauce, and coarsely diced all the vegetables.
2. Stir them properly, adding more water for liquid as necessary.
3. Create circular balls from the thick vegetable mixture.
4. Now deep fry the vegetable balls in a pot.
5. In a skillet, warm some oil and cook it with garlic, ginger, and green chili for a moment.
6. Add black pepper, green onions, tomato sauce, chili sauce, sesame oil, and seasoning.
7. Put them together well and transfer to the pan with a mixture of corn flour containing water.
8. Thoroughly combine and bring the balls of fried vegetables into the solution.
9. Place the balls together with the sauce well.
10. Garnish with green onion and celery.

Honey Chili Potato Recipe

Cooking Time: 40 minutes

Serving Size: 4

Ingredients:

- Oil for deep frying
- 4-5 potatoes

First Coating

- 3 tablespoons all-purpose flour
- 2 teaspoon salt
- 1 teaspoon red chili paste
- 3 tablespoon cornflour
- 1 teaspoon garlic paste
- 2 teaspoon chili powder

Second Coating

- ¼ teaspoon black pepper
- 2-3 tablespoon water
- 3 tablespoons all-purpose flour
- 3 tablespoon cornflour

For the Sauce

- ¼ cup water
- 2 tablespoon spring onion
- 1 ½ tablespoon honey
- 1 teaspoon red chili paste
- 1 teaspoon soy sauce
- 2 tablespoon tomato ketchup
- 2 tablespoon oil
- 3 tablespoon white sesame seeds
- 1 teaspoon vinegar
- 1 teaspoon red chili flakes
- 1 tablespoon garlic

Method:

1. Wash the potato fingers well enough and set them aside in clean water. Keeping in water extracts all excess starch from the potatoes.

2. Combine the chili paste, cornmeal, chili powder, all-purpose flour, and salt along.

3. With this flour combination, cover the potato fingers uniformly.

4. Heat the oil in a pan or skillet and fry the potato fingers in groups until the potato is half fried.

5. It is essential to put one potato finger in the oil at the moment not to bind together.

6. On a tissue-lined tray, extract the potato fingers and allow them to clear.

7. Create a moderate mixture of all-purpose flour, cornmeal and peppers paste for the second covering by applying only a few tablespoons.

8. In this mixture, insert the half-finished fries and fry them once more in hot oil until crisp and yellow.

9. In a pan, heat two teaspoons oil, add minced cloves and reheat for a few seconds.

10. To top them, add sesame seeds and chili flakes and sauté for the next two minutes.

11. Then include the mustard, lime juice, ketchup, soy sauce, and red chili paste and blend well.

12. To make a liquid, combine cornstarch with ¼ cup water and insert this into the wok's combination and stir for the next few seconds before it hardens.

13. Insert the fried potato fingers and green onion leaves and toss them together till they are uniformly covered in liquid.

14. Turn the flame off and quickly serve.

Veg Hakka Noodles

Cooking Time: 25 minutes

Serving Size: 3

Ingredients:

- Pinch white pepper powder
- 1 teaspoon chili oil optional
- ¼ teaspoon black pepper powder
- ½ teaspoon salt
- 1 teaspoon hot sauce Sriracha
- ½ teaspoon sugar
- 300 grams noodles
- 2.5 tablespoons soy sauce
- 1 tablespoon rice vinegar
- 1 large red pepper 200 grams
- 1 red onion 100 grams
- 1 large carrot 100 grams, sliced
- 3 stalks green onion
- 1 green chili sliced
- 1 stalk celery chopped
- 2 teaspoons minced garlic
- 1 teaspoon minced ginger
- 1 tablespoon vegetable oil
- 1 tablespoon sesame oil

Method:

1. Once you start preparing the pasta, cut all the vegetables.

2. Cook the pasta as per the package directions.

3. Wash the paste and rinse them under cold water, which prevents the phase of over-cooking.

4. Transfer the pasta to a half tablespoon of cooking oil and mix to brush with the oil finely and do not let it cling together. Set aside.

5. Heat two tablespoons of cooking oil and one tablespoon of sesame oil in a skillet over medium to high flame.

6. Insert the diced ginger and garlic, the sliced green pepper, and the diced celery when the oil is warmed.

7. Sauté the garlic ginger for several seconds before it begins to change color.

8. Insert the chopped onion and sauté until the onion surfaces begin to turn golden yellow-brown for a couple of minutes.

9. Insert the diced peppers, carrots, and spring onions and simmer over high heat for two minutes. They should keep crunchy with the vegetables.

10. Turn the heat down and apply soy sauce, rice wine vinegar, sweet sauce, and sugar.

11. To mix well with the liquid, flip the vegetables. Add cinnamon, red pepper, and white pepper.

12. Mix in the pasta that has been cooked. Shake it well with a pair of chopsticks, ensuring that the pasta is well mixed with the liquid.

13. Mix in teaspoons of chili oil as a finishing pass. This is voluntary too.

14. Toss the pasta well and incorporate more green onion leaves to flavor.

Vegetable Chopsuey Recipe

Cooking Time: 50 minutes

Serving Size: 2

Ingredients:

- 2 tablespoon cornflour
- Oil
- ½ Cup carrots
- 1 teaspoon sugar
- Salt
- 1 cup cabbage
- 2 tablespoon vinegar
- ½ teaspoon soya sauce
- 2 tablespoon oil
- 200 grams noodles
- ½ cup capsicums
- 2 teaspoon garlic
- ½ cup onions

Method:

1. Combine the vinegar, sugar, soy sauce, flour, and salt.
2. Pour sufficient water, and prepare a bowl. Set it aside.
3. Heat two tablespoons of oil and add the onions and garlic.
4. Sauté before relatively gentle.
5. For a moment, add the vegetables, capsicum, and cabbage and stir-fry over medium temperature.
6. Transfer the liquid solution and fry, constantly stirring. Put it back.
7. On high flame, pan-fry the pasta until brown.
8. Move the pasta to a serving platter, spill over the veggies and eat.

Crunchy Iceberg Dumpling

Cooking Time: 45 minutes

Serving Size: 3

Ingredients:

- Salt - as per taste
- Wheat starch and water
- 10 grams asparagus
- 5 ml sesame oil
- 5 ml ginger juice
- 10 grams water chestnut
- 10 grams iceberg lettuce roughly
- 5 grams sugar
- 10 grams red pumpkin
- 10 grams raw papaya

- 10 grams corn kernel

Method:

1. Caramelize all the veggies along, excluding the iceberg.
2. Cook the stuffing and leave it aside until it is set.
3. To shape the filling, combine the remaining ingredients with the caramelized veggies.
4. To create a batter, prepare the skin by using grain starch and liquid.
5. Break and divide the crust into equal parts to make a wrap using a wheel.
6. Insert the filling into the dumplings and cover.
7. Serve it hot.

Chinese Broccoli with Orange

Cooking Time: 25 minutes

Serving Size: 4

Ingredients:

Orange Sauce

- 3 tablespoon cornstarch
- 3 tablespoon water
- 2 cloves garlic, minced
- ½ teaspoon red pepper flakes
- 1-2 tablespoon brown sugar
- 1 teaspoon minced ginger
- ½ - ¾ cup orange juice
- ¼ cup soy sauce
- ¼ cup rice vinegar
- 1 teaspoon orange zest

Seitan

- Sesame seeds
- Jasmine rice, to serve
- ½ tablespoon oil
- 2 scallions, sliced
- 8oz seitan or vegan meat
- ¼ teaspoon white pepper
- 2 tablespoon cornstarch
- ¼ teaspoon salt
- 1 crown broccoli
- 1 tablespoon soy sauce
- ¼ teaspoon white pepper
- ½ tablespoon oil
- Broccoli
- 1 tablespoon cornstarch

Method:

1. Except for cornflour and water, combine all the sauce components, beginning with two tablespoons of brown sugar.

2. If needed, try and add further sugar.

3. In a small dish, mix the cornflour and water once applying to the sauce. Mix to blend.

4. Swirl the Seitan with the pepper and salt in a dish, then mix it with cornflour to cover.

5. Mix the broccoli in a small bowl of soy sauce and peppers and then insert the cornflour and mix until the broccoli is covered.

6. Steam in a skillet or pan over moderate to high heat.

7. Add a dash of oil and the seitan once it has been warmed.

8. Cook for four minutes or until tender, almost continually mixing. Remove from the heat.

9. Insert a small amount of oil as well as the broccoli.

10. Cook for four minutes and add the light green and white parts of the chopped spring onions until the broccoli is dark green and turns soft.

11. Cook for another thirty seconds.

12. Together with the gravy, transfer seitan straight to the pan.

13. Simmer the liquid and then let it steam and thicken for around two minutes before the seitan and broccoli are thickly coated.

14. Serve with rice noodles right away and garnish with spring onion greens and pumpkin seeds.

Vegan Chinese Vegetable and Seitan Stir-Fry Recipe

Cooking Time: 25 minutes

Serving Size: 4

Ingredients:

- 1 red or yellow bell pepper
- 1 cups broccoli
- 1 cups seitan
- 2 green onions
- 3 tablespoon hoisin sauce
- 1 teaspoon fresh ginger
- 1 tablespoon corn starch
- ¾ cups vegetable broth

- 2 cloves garlic
- 1 tablespoon sesame oil
- 1 tablespoon rice vinegar
- 2 tablespoon sugar
- 2 tablespoon soy sauce

Method:

1. Firstly, mix the sauce for your stir-fry.

Mix all the hoisin sauces and one tablespoon oil with two tablespoon sesame in a shallow frying pan over medium flame.

2. Mix rice, vinegar, soy sauce, vegetable broth, cinnamon, ginger, garlic, and cornstarch.

3. Bring it to boil for around five minutes or so, then remove from heat and set it aside until the mixture starts to stiffen.

4. Stir-fry the seitan in two tablespoons of oil in a large wok or pan and fry until soy sauce is browned gently for about four minutes.

5. Insert the onions, broccoli, and peppers and stir-fry for three minutes.

6. While stir-frying, insert the cooked stir-fry liquid mixture and blend well, leaving 2-3 further cooking minutes until broccoli is cooked.

7. Serve over fried rice or pasta, if you prefer, or simply with boiled white rice or your choice of whole grain with your Chinese vegetable stir-fry.

Chapter 3: Chinese Vegetarian Breakfast and Snack Recipes

3.1 Vegetarian Breakfasts Recipes

Vegetarian Baozi

Cooking Time: 1 hour 25 minutes

Serving Size: 4

Ingredients:

For the Dough

- 1 tablespoon cooking oil
- Instant yeast 2¼ teaspoons
- 160 grams water
- 300 grams all-purpose flour

For the Fillings

- 1 teaspoon salt
- 1 teaspoon light soy sauce
- 1-inch ginger
- 1 teaspoon cooking oil
- 1 teaspoon doubanjiang
- 1 garlic clove
- 1 tablespoon spring onions
- 1 box of regular tofu

Method:

1. Prepare hot water at about 35 °C
2. Together with the water, combine the yeast. Shake well and put aside for five minutes or more.

3. In a wide pan, mix the flour.

4. Slowly add the liquid with the yeast into a bowl of flour and mix with the spoon.

5. Knead the dry ingredients into a soft, smooth mixture.

6. Cover the pan and allow the dough to rest for about two hours until the mix ball's size increases.

7. Have the mixing ball out until the dough is doubled in thickness.

8. Now, roll the dough about 2 inches in diameter or whatever size you like into a long stick.

9. On your table, sprinkle some flour and break the stick into tiny pieces about 1 inch long.

10. With thin sides, roll the tiny bread into a round wrapping.

11. Heat the pan with frying oil.

12. First of all, stir fry garlic, ginger, and doubanjiang.

13. With salts and mild soy sauce, incorporate the scrambled tofu. Mix thoroughly.

14. Take the saucepan from the flame and combine the sliced green onions. Shape the baozi.

15. Rub the base of each baozi with some oil and bring it into the container.

16. Warm up the wok's liquid and start steaming.

17. Count at least a few minutes after the liquid starts to boil in the wok. Serve warm.

Pancakes (Jian Bing)

Cooking Time: 30 minutes

Serving Size: 4

Ingredients:

For the Crackers

- Cooking oil
- 16 ready-made wonton wrappers

For the Batter

- 300 ml water
- 40 grams whole meal flour
- 70 grams all-purpose flour

For the Crepes

- 4 teaspoons finely chopped scallions
- 4 eggs
- 4 teaspoon toasted sesame seeds

For the Sauce

- 4 teaspoon soybean paste
- 4 teaspoon chili garlic sauce

Optional

- Lettuce leaves
- Coriander

Method:

1. Brush the wonton wrapping with a thin film of water.
2. To close, press gently. Stick a few on edge and then use a spatula.

3. Split the two lines in the center. To create more than seven sets, replicate.

4. In a wok, heat the oil. Begin cooking when the temperature exceeds 180°C.

5. Slide softly into the wonton wrapping. Switch the other half over to cook.

6. Take out when they are slightly orange. To extract any extra oil, move it to a tray covered with paper towels.

7. In a mixing pot, combine whole meal flour and all-purpose flour. Pour the water in. Mix until clear.

8. Steam a non-stick deep fryer over moderate flame.

9. Pour ¼ of the mixture in when it is hot to touch.

10. Shift the skillet to enable the mixture to cover the whole surface evenly.

11. Crack the egg on top if there are no runny batters, which can be seen. To crack the yolk, just use a slotted spoon to stretch it out.

12. Use scallions and sesame seeds to spread.

13. It is time to turn it over as the crepe gets solid and slips quickly in the bowl.

14. Flip the crepe onto the back edge of a broad lid to prevent tearing, then bring it back into the bowl.

15. While tossing, turn the flame off. Rub the crepe with soybean mixture and hot garlic sauce.

16. If required, add cilantro and chopped lettuce. In the center, put a couple of crispy crackers. After sealing, serve instantly.

Chinese Breakfast Porridge

Cooking Time: 1 hour 35 minutes

Serving Size: 2

Ingredients:

- 1 small sweet potato
- 1 small bunch of collard greens
- ½ cup shiitake mushrooms
- ½ cup dried mixed mushrooms
- 1 cup brown short grain rice
- 1 small knob of ginger
- 4 cups vegetable broth

Topping Suggestions

- Green onions
- Kimchi
- Hot chili oil
- Soy sauce or tamari

Method:

1. Wash and drain the rice properly.
2. Add the vegetable stock, rice or liquid, and ginger into a big pot.
3. Take to a boil, then switch down the temperature and cook, sealed, periodically moving.
4. Meanwhile, when the rice is frying, rinse the dried mushrooms in four cups of hot water in a large pan.
5. Peel and slice the sweet potato into 1-inch pieces. Put aside.
6. Clean and slice the green beans, extracting any rough stalks into 1-inch pieces and put aside.

7. Transfer the mushrooms to the mixture after the congee (porridge) has been cooked for thirty minutes, and the mushrooms are thoroughly mixed with water.

8. Put in the absorbing liquid gently, removing the last fluid where it might have collected some soil and dust.

9. Give the sweet potatoes a swirl. Cover them and keep boiling for another thirty minutes, stirring regularly.

10. Whisk in the green beans after thirty minutes. Continue to cook for a further fifteen minutes, stirring regularly.

11. The rice grains should have completely wilted and absorbed much of the moisture at this stage.

12. If the congee is too runny, boil to allow any steam to discharge, over the last fifteen minutes without covering the bowl.

13. If the congee is too dense, excess water may be inserted as required.

Chicken Mustard Green Congee

Cooking Time: 55 minutes

Serving Size: 2

Ingredients:

- ½ teaspoon dark soy sauce
- ¼ cup finely chopped chives
- ¼ cup preserved mustard greens
- 1 tablespoon sesame oil
- 12 oz. chicken tenderloin
- 2 crushed garlic cloves
- ¾ cup sweet rice
- 1 ginger peeled and sliced

Method:

1. Add rice, four cups of water, garlic, and ginger in a kettle. Just get it to a boil.

2. Add the chicken, boil, and prepare for about twenty minutes until the chicken is fully cooked.

3. Strain and reserve the fluid. As soon as it is cold enough to hold the chicken, slice it by hand.

4. Mix the chicken, ginger, and four cups of water in a big bowl. Just get it to a boil.

5. Boil and heat for about fifteen minutes, till the chicken is thoroughly cooked. Put the herb away.

6. Shred the chicken by fingers, as fast as it is cold enough to treat.

7. To make six cups, transfer water to the filtered broth.

8. Mix six cups of broth-water with rice in a bowl. Just get it to a boil.

9. Simmer the paste, cover the pot for thirty minutes.

10. Add the chicken, green beans, sesame oil, soy sauce, and chives.

11. Cook for five minutes over medium temperature.

12. When served, cover and allow to sit for ten minutes.

Breakfast Noodle Bowl

Cooking Time: 40 minutes

Serving Size: 4

Ingredients:

- 1 tablespoon vegan mayo
- 1 cup chopped kale
- 1 tablespoon tofu seasoning
- 1-2 green onions chopped
- 1 serving soba noodles
- ½ tablespoon vegan butter
- 100 grams medium-firm tofu

For the Sauce

- 1 tablespoon agave
- 1 tablespoon rice vinegar
- ½ teaspoon ground ginger
- 1 teaspoon garlic powder
- 1 tablespoon soy sauce

Method:

1. In a kettle, begin boiling water. You should begin preparing your scrambling tofu when looking for the water to boil.

2. In a skillet, heat some vegetable oil.

3. If the pot has warmed up a little, by cracking with your side, bring in the tofu.

4. Enable it to bake on one surface until it is translucent.

5. For added creaminess and flavor, incorporate a little touch of vegan mayo. Mix thoroughly.

6. Add spices to the tofu scrambled and blend until all the bits of tofu are well-coated. Put aside.

7. When the water begins to boil, insert the soba noodles and enable them to cook for five minutes.

8. Put in the kale while the soba noodles are about two steps away from being finished.

9. Discharge the kale and noodles and wash under cool water.

10. Place the components in the sauce into a container. Mix thoroughly.

11. Cover with fried tofu and spring onions, sliced. Sprinkle before eating with organic mayo.

Spicy Asian Breakfast Crepes

Cooking Time: 30 minutes

Serving Size: 4

Ingredients:

- 1 (3.5-oz) package wonton strips
- Sriracha hot sauce
- 8 teaspoon chile-garlic sauce

- ¾ cup drained kimchi
- Canola oil
- 2 tablespoon sesame seeds
- 8 teaspoon hoisin sauce
- 8- 10-inch French-style crepes
- 2 bunches of green onions
- 1 cup cilantro leaves
- 4 large eggs

Method:

1. Heat the oven to 200 degrees F. Place the baking sheet.

2. Over moderate flame, heat a large broiler pan or grill pan. Clean with oil gently.

3. Put two crepes in a tray and stack them. Insert one-quarter of the eggs and scatter to cover the crepe top.

4. Spray with ¼ of an onion, ¼ of a cup of coriander, and 1 ½ teaspoon of sesame seeds.

5. Cook for two minutes or until the egg is firm.

6. Flip and push down with a spoon on the back. Roll one-third of the ground up.

7. Cover with two teaspoons of chili-garlic sauce and two teaspoons of hoisin.

8. Cover with three tablespoons of kimchi and strips of around 1/3 cup of the wonton.

9. Fold back, Fold it up. Split crosswise in two.

10. To keep it warm, put it in the oven. Replicate with the rest of the ingredients.

11. Serve, if needed, with Sriracha.

Creamy Wheat Berry Porridge

Cooking Time: 5 minutes

Serving Size: 4-6

Ingredients:

Creamy Berry Porridge:

- 2 tablespoons chia seeds
- 1 tablespoon coconut oil
- ½ teaspoon sea salt
- 2½ cups (590 ml) dairy-free milk
- 4 cups (950 ml) water
- 1 cup (175 g) hard wheat berries

Gingered Blueberry Topping

- ½ teaspoon fresh lemon juice
- ⅛ teaspoon sea salt
- 1 tablespoon water
- ½-inch piece fresh ginger
- 2 tablespoons maple syrup
- 1¼ cups (175 g) frozen blueberries

Other

- Full-fat coconut milk

Method:

1. In a small saucepan, put the wheat berries, liquid, and salts and bring to a simmer.

2. Seal the pot, switch down the flame, and simmer for forty-five minutes, mixing occasionally.

3. Turn the heat down and allow the porridge to stay for an hour.

4. Bring to a boil over a moderate flame, mix in chia seeds, milk, and coconut oil.

5. Take off the heat, cover and allow to rest for ten minutes before serving.

6. In the meantime, over a moderate flame, mix all the coating components in a shallow saucepan.

7. Close the frying pan, bring it to a simmer, and cook it for three minutes, changing the heat if needed to keep it from boiling over. Serve immediately.

Zen Quinoa Bowl

Cooking Time: 15 minutes

Serving Size: 1

Ingredients:

- ¼ avocado, sliced
- ¼ cup deli sprouts
- 1 lime, halved
- ¼ teaspoon salt
- ⅛ teaspoon pepper
- ¼ teaspoon onion powder
- ¼ teaspoon paprika
- ½ cup cooked quinoa
- ½ teaspoon yellow curry powder
- ¼ teaspoon garlic powder
- 6 egg whites
- 1 cup kale, torn into pieces
- ½ cup carrot, grated
- ½ cup chopped broccoli

- ¼ cup mushrooms, sliced
- ¼ cup cherry tomatoes halved

Method:

1. Place a wok or casserole dish over moderate to low heat.

2. Mix the ingredients in a shallow saucepan and add salt and pepper.

3. Add broccoli, mushrooms, carrots, and a bit of water while the wok is warm and simmer for four minutes before the vegetable becomes tender.

4. In the broccoli and grape tomatoes, add spice blend.

5. Reduce the heat to mild.

6. Keep sautéing till the broccoli is shrunken, and insert little swirls of water as required so that the veggies do not stick or smoke.

7. Try squeezing half of the lemon juice and mix in the egg whites.

8. Enable the egg whites to stay before they start frying, then mix them along with the veggies for a moment.

9. When the eggs are thoroughly cooked, pass the combination to a quinoa pan and pour this with the quinoa.

10. Cover the combination of vegetables with sprouts and sliced avocado and, if needed, garnish with another slice of lime and some extra black pepper.

Vermicelli Noodle Bowl

Cooking Time: 10 minutes

Serving Size: 4

Ingredients:

- Coriander leaves
- 5 tablespoon roasted peanuts
- ¼ cup coconut milk
- Lime juice
- 1 teaspoon ginger grated
- 2 tablespoon Sriracha sauce hot sauce
- 2 tablespoon soy sauce
- 1.5 cup water
- Salt to taste
- 1 teaspoon chili powder
- 1 onion small
- 1 tablespoon Oil
- 1 cup Vermicelli pasta
- 2-3 green chili
- ½ cup Mushroom chopped
- ½ cup Corn kernels frozen
- ½ bell peppers

Method:

1. In a skillet, add the oil and insert the sliced onions, sliced green chili and sauté.

2. Insert the sliced mushrooms, bell peppers, maize, and sauté for three minutes over moderate flame.

3. Transfer noodles to vermicelli and blend properly.

4. Add cinnamon, red chili flakes, soy sauce, Sriracha sauce, and spice.

5. Insert 1.5 cups of almond milk and water.

6. Mix properly, turn down the heat after it boils and cook on medium heat for five minutes.

7. Transfer sliced baby tomatoes and toasted oats.

8. Garnish with lemon juice, baked peanuts, and cilantro leaves in a dish and serve warm.

3.2 Vegetarian Snacks Recipes

Veg Lollipop Recipe

Cooking Time: 30 minutes

Serving Size: 12

Ingredients:

- White pepper
- Salt to taste
- 2 teaspoons green chilly
- 2 tablespoon schezwan sauce
- 3 cups cabbage
- 2 tablespoon cornflour
- 1 tablespoon garlic
- ½ tablespoon ginger
- 14 cup carrot, grated
- ¼ cup onion
- Few beans

Method:

1. Stir together all the veggies, except the onion.
2. Sprinkle the salt.
3. Shake well after five minutes and strain the extra water away.
4. Add all ingredients into the mixture.
5. If necessary, add water.
6. Create the balls of dough and deep-fry them.
7. Serve in sauces with cloves.

Air-Fried Crispy Vegetables

Cooking Time: 15 minutes

Serving Size: 2

Ingredients:

- 2 cups mixed vegetables

For Batter

- 1 teaspoon salt
- 1 teaspoon oil
- ½-1 teaspoon red chili powder
- ½-1 teaspoon black pepper powder
- ½ teaspoon garlic powder
- ¼ cup all-purpose flour
- ¼ cup cornstarch

For Sauce Mix

- 1 tablespoon vinegar
- 1 teaspoon brown sugar
- 1 tablespoon chili sauce

- 1 tablespoon tomato ketchup
- 2 tablespoon soy sauce

Other

- 1 teaspoon sesame seeds
- spring onion greens for garnish
- 1 tablespoon sesame oil

Method:

1. Cut the cauliflower into tiny florets, cut the bell peppers into balls, cut the mushroom in two, and cut the zucchini and carrots into rings.

2. Do not cut very short slices.

3. Create a mixture of all-purpose flour, garlic powder, bell pepper powder, cornstarch, red chili powder, and salt.

4. Take a fluffy lump-free batter by inserting a teaspoon of oil.

5. Transfer all the veggies and coat them well in the batter.

6. Heat the air fryer to 350F, then, as suggested, add the vegetables.

7. It takes several minutes for the vegetables to air fry.

8. Create a mixed sauce.

9. Heat a tablespoon of oil in a heavy-bottomed pot, add coarsely diced garlic. Sauté until it gives flavor, then insert sauce mixture and cracked black pepper.

10. Insert the air-fried veggies and blend well with light hands. Steam for a moment.

11. Cover all the vegetables in a spicy seasoning.

12. Sprinkle with sesame oil and green onions leaves, coarsely diced, and serve soft.

13. Combine all the ingredients mentioned in the portion of the sauce simultaneously.

14. Cover the veggies well in the mixture and then fry them deep in hot oil until lighter shades.

15. The oil should be warm enough to keep the vegetables crispy.

16. Take it out, cool it off, and apply sauces mixture to it.

Idli Manchurian

Cooking Time: 20 minutes

Serving Size: 2

Ingredients:

For Pan Frying Idli

- 2 tablespoons oil
- 5 medium to large idlis

Other Ingredients

- Salt as required
- 2 tablespoons coriander leaves
- ½ tablespoon red chili sauce
- ¼ teaspoon black pepper powder
- 1 tablespoon soy sauce
- ½ tablespoon sweet red chili sauce
- 1 medium onion
- 1 small capsicum
- 1 tablespoon oil
- 1 teaspoon ginger
- 1 teaspoon ginger
- 1.5 teaspoon garlic

Method:

1. In a small saucepan or skillet, heat two tablespoons of olive oil. Switch on a moderate flame and put the idlis in place.
2. Switch over the idlis once a part is crispy and translucent and the second part is fried.
3. Also, fry the double side of the idlis until they become crispy and translucent.
4. Put the skillet fried idlis on cooking towels. Let a few of them cool.
5. Once the idlis are mildly hot, cut four sections of them.
6. In a pot or skillet, heat one tablespoon of olive oil.
7. Add coarsely diced ginger, garlic, and green chili, thinly sliced.
8. Sauté before the garlic begins to turn brightly golden on medium heat.
9. Then substitute the vegetables and capsicum that have been sliced.
10. On a moderate to high flame, blend and start sautéing the onions and bell pepper, moving sometimes.
11. Sauté until both the onions and pepper edges are softly translucent with any blisters on both.
12. Retain the flame down and apply one tablespoon of soy sauce.
13. Add half a tablespoon of chili flakes sauce or Sriracha sauce instantly.
14. Then include half of a tablespoon of mild red chili or tomato sauce.

15. Blend quite well.

16. Then insert ¼ teaspoon of powdered black pepper.

17. As needed, add some salt and combine again.

18. As the sauces still have salt in them, add less salt. Blend very well.

19. Then insert the pan-fried Idlis.

20. Mix enough that the idlis are filled with the sauces. Turn the flame off.

21. Finally, add two teaspoons of chopped cilantro leaves. Then, blend.

22. Cold or hot, eat idli Manchurian as a quick snack.

Veggie Scallion Pancakes

Cooking Time: 1 hour 14 minutes

Serving Size: 4

Ingredients:

- Peanut oil
- 1 cup chopped scallions
- 1 tablespoon toasted sesame oil
- ¾ cup just-boiled water
- ¾ teaspoon salt
- 1 ¾ cup all-purpose flour

For the Sauce

- ½ teaspoon toasted sesame oil
- ½ teaspoon sambal oelek
- 2 tablespoons rice vinegar
- 3 tablespoons soy sauce

For Serving

- **Toasted sesame seeds**

Method:

1. In a wide blending cup, mix the salt and flour.

2. Insert hot water and sesame oil. To shape a shaggy mixture, stir all together.

3. Pour the mixture onto a gently floured surface and whisk for approximately 3 minutes, until soft.

4. Roll it into a shape with the dough.

5. With a tablespoon or three of oil, gently scrub the dough and pass it to a dry pan.

6. With a moist rag, coat the dough and then let it sit for thirty minutes.

7. Create the sauces by mixing all the components in a shallow saucepan as the dough sits.

8. Split it into four equal parts after the dough has settled.

9. Remove one part of the bowl's dough and obtain the remaining.

10. Position the dough section on a thinly floured surface and shape it into a nearly 6-inch ring using a spoon.

11. Rub the dough gently with oil and season the shallots with it.

12. Firmly roll the dough into a long snake like shape, enveloping the scallions inside. Coil the serpent into a coil.

13. Form the coil into a small seven to eight-inch circle with your rolling pin.

14. With a wet cloth, protect the dough circle, and repeat the procedure with the dough's remaining portions.

15. Use kitchen towels between each one, pile the assembled dough spheres, and protect them with a damp cloth.

16. Cover the large pan's bottom adequately with roughly two to three tablespoons of oil and put over a moderate fire.

17. To heat it, leave the oil a moment, then move one of your bread rings to your pan.

18. On either hand, cook for around three minutes, until golden brown and translucent.

19. Switch the fried pancake to a sheet lined with paper towels and repeat the procedure with the dough's leftover circles.

20. Cut and slice your spring onion pancakes while they are sweet, with dripping sauce on top, preferably topped with sesame oil.

Chinese Salt and Pepper Tofu

Cooking Time: 50 minutes

Serving Size: 2

Ingredients:

For the Sauté

- 1 tablespoon light soy sauce
- ½ teaspoon brown sugar
- 1 tablespoon garlic
- 1 tablespoon finely minced ginger
- 1 celery rib
- 1 small green pepper
- 2 medium leeks
- ½ tablespoon oil

For the Tofu

- Freshly cracked black pepper
- Salt
- 1 block extra firm tofu
- ½ teaspoon or to taste
- 4 tablespoons corn starch

Method:

1. To make a fine dice, cut the leeks, celery, and bell pepper.
2. Heat the oil over the moderate flame in a skillet.
3. Add the chopped green pepper, leeks, and celery.
4. Sauté for around two minutes under high pressure. Add ginger and garlic.
5. Cook for two minutes again. Insert the soy and brown sugar mixture and simmer for thirty seconds. Set aside the combination.
6. Clean the washed tofu. Split into cubes of around 1 inch.
7. In a wide bowl, put the tofu blocks.
8. Transform corn starch, black pepper, and salt.
9. Gently toss until the bits of tofu are quite well covered.
10. Pour oil into a pan until it goes up to ½ inch. Make sure that the oil is warm.
11. Insert few tofu pieces at once.
12. If you cook so many of them in one go, they are not going to crisp up.
13. Toss them over, fry the tofu bits so that both surfaces are nicely browned.

14. The sautéed celery, leeks, and green pepper can be heated up. Insert cubes of fried tofu into it.

15. Serve with your hot sauce with vegetarian Chinese seasoning and pepper and season with celery sticks or spring onions.

Chapter 4: Chinese Famous Vegetarian Recipes

4.1 Vegetarian Soup Recipes

Vegetarian Hot and Sour Soup

Cooking Time: 1 hour 20 minutes

Serving Size: 8

Ingredients:

- 1 large egg (beaten)
- 1 scallion (chopped)
- ¼-1/3 cup white vinegar
- ¼ cup cornstarch
- 0.35 oz. lily flowers
- 1 teaspoon sesame oil
- 5 oz. bamboo shoots
- 0.35 oz. wood ear mushrooms (½ cup)
- 1 ½ teaspoons mushroom dark soy sauce
- 1 tablespoon light soy sauce
- 0.7 oz. shiitake mushrooms (⅔ cup)
- 3 oz. spiced dry tofu
- 1-2 dried red chili peppers
- 1-2 teaspoons white pepper
- 4 oz. fresh firm tofu
- ½ teaspoon salt
- ¼ teaspoon sugar

- 7 cups vegetable stock

Method:

1. Add water in small pots, and wash the dried lily plants, wood ear mushrooms, and shiitake mushrooms.

2. Set aside the shiitake mushrooms soaked in liquid.

3. Cut the lily plants off the rough edges and split them in half.

4. Cut the wood ear mushroom finely, then break the shiitake mushrooms finely.

5. Cut the flavored tofu into thinly sliced ranging two inches in thickness.

6. Cut the tofu, about two inches long, into ¼ inch thick bits.

7. In a wide fry pan, add the stock and drained mushrooms soaked in broth, and bring it to a boil.

8. Add white pepper, cinnamon, chili pepper, sugar, heavy soy sauce, sesame oil, and mild soy sauce, if necessary.

9. Then, insert the lily plants, wood ear mushrooms, bamboo shoots, and shiitake mushrooms.

10. Take the soup to a boil, and mix in the flavored tofu, strong tofu, and cider.

11. Mix the cornflour to produce a liquid with ¼ cup of water.

12. As the cornflour appears to accumulate at the bottom of the dish, make sure it is well-combined.

13. To create a whirlpool while gently raining in the cornflour sludge, bring the mixture to a boil and use the broth skillet to whisk the soup in a slow clockwise direction. It avoids the clogging of the cornstarch.

14. To thicken, boil for the next thirty seconds.

15. Flavor the soup and adjust to your choice of spices. If you want a spicier flavour, add extra pepper.

16. Some liquor, sesame oil, or salt can be added as well.

17. Mix the broth in a circular motion once more, with the liquid bubbling slightly.

18. Load the egg mixture gently in a fine mist into the soup.

19. Insert the green onion when the eggs are fried, and consume!

Chinese Vegetable Soup

Cooking Time: 20 minutes

Serving Size: 2

Ingredients:

- Salt and black pepper to taste
- Green onions for garnish
- 1 head of bok choy, sliced
- 1 teaspoon of sesame oil
- 4 cups of vegetable broth
- 1 carrot, sliced
- 3-4 cloves of garlic, minced
- 2 tablespoons of soy sauce
- 2-3 sprigs of cilantro
- 1-inch ginger, chopped
- 1 cup of mushroom, sliced

Method:

1. In a pan, take the liquid to a boil.

2. Turn the heat down and transfer the diced mushrooms, garlic, ginger, coriander, bok choy and diced carrots.

3. Mix in the liquid of soy. Use salts and finely ground black pepper to spice.

4. Cook for about seven minutes before the bok choy lightens.

5. Spoon into pots; glaze and top with sesame oil.

Vegetarian Dan Dan Noodle Soup

Cooking Time: 15 minutes

Serving Size: 4

Ingredients:

Stock

- 2 teaspoon minced ginger
- 2 teaspoon sugar
- 4 cups vegetable stock
- 3 large garlic cloves, minced
- 5 cups water

Stock Sauce

- 2 teaspoon chili bean sauce
- 1 ½ teaspoon sesame oil
- 2 tablespoon sesame paste
- 4 tablespoons black vinegar
- 2 teaspoon cornflour
- 3 tablespoon soy sauce

Garnish

- 1 scallion, chopped

- 1 ½ cups bean sprouts

Toppings

- 2 medium carrots
- 2 cups broccoli florets
- 4 bok choy

Method:

1. In a wide bowl, mix the stock components and bring them to a boil.

2. In the meantime, in a small bowl, combine the broth sauce components and split all the veggies into bite-size parts.

3. Transfer the stock liquid and blend deep into the broth to absorb. As needed, change the spice.

4. Put the rice sticks pasta in the stock once the mixture comes to a simmer, then insert the broccoli and carrot one moment later, remove them from the flame one minute later and insert the bok choy ends.

5. Divide into containers, cover with bok choy leaf and black beans, pasta, and veggies.

6. Spoon the veggies and pasta into bowls of soup, and garnish with green onions.

Vegetable Manchow Soup Recipe

Cooking Time: 35 minutes

Serving Size: 4

Ingredients:

For Fried Noodles

- 1 teaspoon cornflour

- oil, for frying
- 1 teaspoon oil
- 1 pack Hakka noodles
- 1 teaspoon salt
- 4 cup water

For Soup

- ¼ cup water, for slurry
- 2 tablespoon coriander
- 1 teaspoon chili sauce
- 1 teaspoon cornflour
- 2 tablespoon oil
- 2 tablespoon vinegar
- ½ teaspoon pepper powder
- 1-inch ginger
- ¾ teaspoon salt
- 2 tablespoon soy sauce
- 2 clove garlic
- 2 chilies, chopped
- 2 tablespoon coriander stem
- 4 cup water
- ½ onion, chopped
- ½ capsicum, chopped
- 5 beans, chopped
- ½ carrot, chopped
- 3 tablespoon cabbage, chopped

Method:

1. Firstly, place four cups of water, one teaspoon of salt, and one teaspoon of oil in a wide pot.

2. Crush 1 pack of Hakka pasta until the liquid begins to boil.

3. To understand the preparation temperature, boil for five minutes or respond to product instructions.

4. Cook before the al dente pasta transforms without over-heating.

5. When finished, rinse the pasta and clean them with water.

6. Then add one teaspoon of cornstarch and softly mash it up.

7. In warm oil, deep-fried by distributing the noodles thinly.

8. Stir from time to time, holding flame on moderate.

9. Switch all sides over and fry until the noodles become crisp.

10. Eventually, the crispy pasta is drained away and held aside.

11. Next, heat two teaspoons of oil, sauté one inch of garlic, ginger, and two chilies in a broad wok.

12. Sauté ½ onion as well, until it shrinks a bit.

13. Then add ½ onion, three tablespoons of cabbage, five peas, ½ bell pepper, and two tablespoons of cilantro stem.

14. Avoid over-frying, stir fry for a moment.

15. Then pour four cups of water, then add ¾ teaspoons of salt. Mix thoroughly.

16. Boil until sufficiently saturated in all the flavors.

17. Then add two teaspoons of soy sauce, half teaspoon of chili powder, two tablespoons of vinegar, and one teaspoon of chili sauce. Mix thoroughly.

18. Take one teaspoon of cornstarch in a large mixing bowl and mix it with half a cup of water.

19. Load the sludge on the cornflour and mix well.

20. Mix and simmer until the broth becomes shiny and softens slightly.

21. Add two teaspoons of cilantro to make it a nice blend.

22. Eventually, enjoy veg Manchow broth with rice noodles served with a mix.

Chinese Vegetable Soup with Tofu

Cooking Time: 20 minutes

Serving Size: 4

Ingredients:

- Salt and white pepper to taste
- Sesame oil
- 3 cups Napa cabbage leaves
- 454 g soft tofu drained
- 7 oz. enoki mushroom
- 3 green onions thinly sliced
- 6 cups water or vegetable stock
- 1 tablespoon olive oil

Method:

1. By wiping some loose soil off with a clean cloth, prepare the enoki mushrooms.
2. Just slice and remove the tips now. Put aside.
3. Turn the heat down in a soup pot over low heat.
4. Reheat the light green pieces of the spring onions for about two minutes until tender.
5. Add more water or stock and turn up the heat to maximum.
6. Get it to a boil with the solution.
7. Add a little salt to the cabbage or bok choy; simmer for around two minutes.
8. Insert the tofu and the enoki mushrooms; cook over medium heat.

9. Add salt and water to your taste.

10. Ladle the broth into a separate pan.

11. Serve with a downpour of soy sauce and finish with spring onions and deep green parts.

4.2 Famous Vegetarian Recipes

Green Beans in Black Bean Sauce

Cooking Time: 30 minutes

Serving Size: 4

Ingredients:

- 2 tablespoon minced ginger
- 1 clove garlic, minced
- 1 lb. haricots verts, trimmed
- Kosher salt
- 1 teaspoon granulated sugar
- 3 tablespoons canola oil
- 1 tablespoon soy sauce
- 1 tablespoon rice vinegar
- 2 teaspoon Asian sesame oil
- 2 tablespoon Chinese black bean sauce

Method:

1. Combine the sesame oil, vinegar, black bean sauce, soy sauce, and sugar in a small cup, and set it aside.

2. Warm the cooking oil over a moderate flame in a wide straight-sided casserole pan until it shimmers.

3. Spray with ¼ of a teaspoon salt, and insert the beans.

4. Simmer for ten minutes, regularly flipping, after most of the beans are golden brown, shortened, and tender.

5. Lower the heat and add the ginger and garlic; simmer for about forty-five seconds.

6. Cook for the next thirty seconds, before the beans are covered, and the liquid is warmed over.

7. Transfer the soy sauce combination to the pot.

Fragrant Eggplant Chinese Vegetarian Recipe

Cooking Time: 1 hour

Serving Size: 4

Ingredients:

- 1 tablespoon Chinkiang vinegar
- 6 tablespoons scallion greens
- 1 teaspoon Chinese light soy sauce
- 10 tablespoons (150ml) hot stock
- 4 teaspoons superfine sugar
- ¾ teaspoon potato starch
- 1 ½ tablespoons garlic
- 1 tablespoon ginger
- 1 pound 5 ounces (600g)
- Cooking oil for deep-frying
- 1 ½ tablespoon Sichuan chili bean paste
- Salt

Method:

1. Break the eggplants into sticks. Season with salt, blend well, and set it aside for thirty minutes or longer.

2. Use towels, clean the eggplant, rinse well enough and dry thoroughly.

3. Heat the deep-frying oil to about 200°C.

4. Insert three or four batches of eggplant and fry for two to three minutes, until soft and a little translucent.

5. Drain on kitchen towels very well and set it aside.

6. Put everything out of the wok except three tablespoons of oil out of the cautiously and switch to medium-high heat.

7. Insert and reheat the chili bean paste till the oil is bright and flavorful: be careful not to burn the sauce.

8. Insert the ginger and garlic and stir-fry until they look tasty.

9. Top in the liquid or stock, sugar, and soy sauce.

10. To enable the eggplant to consume the flavors, simmer for a moment or so.

11. Make the potato grain solution a swirl and steadily substitute it, incorporating just enough to soften the mixture to a lavish liquid in about three phases.

12. Top in the liquor and all but one tablespoon of the spring onion leaves, then swirl to combine the tastes for a few moments.

13. Switch to a serving platter, sprinkle, and serve over the leftover spring onion greens.

Chinese Egg Roll Skins

Cooking Time: 40 minutes

Serving Size: 8

Ingredients:

- ⅞ cup all-purpose flour
- 2 tablespoons peanut oil

- ¾ cup cold water
- ¼ teaspoon salt
- 1 egg, beaten

Method:

1. Mix the egg, salt, and water with each other in a moderate dish.

2. Combine 1/3 at a time with all-purpose flour.

3. Leave the solution to sit at room temperature for fifteen minutes.

4. Over a high flame, steam a skillet.

5. Thinly cover with one tablespoon cooking oil and extract from the heat.

6. Lower the heat to low levels. Place ¼ of the beaten egg into a roughly eight-inch ring while the skillet is still hot.

7. Quickly spin the skillet to disperse an equal coating of batter.

8. Cook for 45 seconds to two minutes over medium heat, until lightly browned on the bottom and the sides start to fold.

9. Remove from the heat cautiously and put upper side down, on a clean cloth.

10. Pour the mixture, ¼ at the moment, the skillet procedure.

11. After the second wrapping has been produced, fry the skillet with the leftover tablespoon of cooking oil.

12. Enable the wrappers to cool. Halve the wrappers to be used in egg rolls.

Fried Potato, Eggplant, and Pepper in Garlic Sauce

Cooking Time: 35 minutes

Serving Size: 4

Ingredients:

Vegetables

- 1 tablespoon tapioca starch
- oil
- 2 medium potatoes
- 1 green capsicum, sliced
- 3 long Asian eggplants

Sauce

- ½ teaspoon white pepper
- 1 tablespoon sesame oil
- 4 tablespoon light soy sauce
- 1 teaspoon sugar
- 1 tablespoon cornstarch
- 2 tablespoon Shaoxing wine
- ¼ cup water

Other

- Salt
- Oil
- 5 cloves garlic, minced
- 3 scallions, chopped

Method:

1. Place the potatoes in a pan and brush them gently with tapioca. Set aside for it.

2. Heat ample oil for pan-frying in a skillet, then deep-fry potatoes until crispy on the bottom. Take the skillet, and set it aside.

3. Quick fry the green capsicums easily until they blister, detach from the skillet, and set it aside.

4. Take all but two tablespoons of oil from the skillet and fry the eggplants on either side until they are finely browned.

5. Then detach it from the skillet and carefully remove it.

6. Mix all the sauce ingredients in a bowl and set them aside.

7. Place the sauce over the same skillet, sauté the scallions and garlic, then let it soften.

8. Insert the veggies and mix, sprinkle with salt, and prepare.

Mu Shu Vegetables Vegetarian Recipe

Cooking Time: 50 minutes

Serving Size: 6-8

Ingredients:

Moo Shu Ingredients

- 1 (14-ounce) bag coleslaw
- ½ cup thinly-sliced green onions
- 8 ounces shiitake mushrooms
- 4 cloves garlic, minced
- 1 batch crispy tofu
- 2 tablespoons peanut oil
- 2 large eggs, whisked
- 1 batch sauce

Sauce Ingredients:

- 1 teaspoon toasted sesame oil
- ¼ teaspoon black pepper
- 2 tablespoons oyster sauce
- 2 tablespoons soy sauce
- ¼ cup rice vinegar
- ½ cup hoisin sauce

Crispy Tofu Ingredients

- ½ teaspoon black pepper
- 1 tablespoon peanut oil
- 2 teaspoons cornstarch
- 1 teaspoon fine sea salt
- 14 ounces extra-firm tofu

For Serving

- Rice or quinoa
- Lettuce cups
- Flour tortillas

Method:

1. Prepare the sauces and crispy tofu.

2. In the meantime, steam two teaspoons of oil over moderate heat in a large non-stick saucepan.

3. Insert the crisped eggs and cook for 2-3 minutes until they are almost fixed and an egg patty is formed.

4. Switch the omelet and bake the second piece for an extra two minutes. Then move the omelet to a different chopping board and slice it into tiny, small strips approximately. Put aside.

5. Transfer the pot to the flame and fire up to a high heat level. Add an extra one tablespoon of oil and steam until it shimmers.

6. Now insert the mushrooms and simmer for four minutes once tender and golden brown, swirling periodically.

7. Insert the Coleslaw and quarter of the green onions. Sauté for an extra three minutes or before the cabbage softens to your taste.

8. Transfer half of the sauce and half of the spring onions to the fried tofu.

9. Toss until they are mixed.

10. If required, flavor and spice with sufficient salt and black pepper.

11. Serve over tortillas of flour, cups of cabbage, corn, or quinoa.

12. Drizzle with the sauces leftover and scatter with the seasonings you like.

13. Cut the tofu cube into ¼-inch wide bricks.

14. On a wide level surface, like a work surface, put several towels or fresh table cloth and place the bricks on the edge of the towels in a flat piece.

15. Cover with some other sheets of towels. Then put a second work surface on top of the tofu, and place on each of the work surfaces a bunch of large pans or pot or something you can comfortably hold.

16. The principle is to place a lot of power on the tofu, which will allow the towels to push out the extra moisture. For a minimum of thirty minutes, let the tofu drain.

17. Bake the tofu in a pan for about 30 minutes until brown.

18. Add the sauces and other mixture.

19. Give a soft shake to the whole mixture and fry for two minutes more, stirring regularly, till the tofu is golden brown to your taste.

20. Switch to a paper plate with the tofu and set it aside until ready.

21. In a small bowl, mix all components until coated.

Asian Red Curry Hot Pot Broth

Cooking Time: 35 minutes

Serving Size: 4

Ingredients:

- 1 teaspoon ginger ground
- 2 tablespoons lime juice
- 1 tablespoon packed light brown sugar
- 1 tablespoon garlic powder
- ¼ cup red curry paste
- 2 tablespoons soy sauce
- 1 large sweet onion
- 2 containers (32 ounces) beef stock
- 2 teaspoons vegetable oil

Method:

1. For the stock, heat the oil across moderate flame in a 6-quart soup pot.

2. Add the onion; continue cooking for about three minutes, till soft.

3. Stir in the stocks, curry paste, soy sauce, garlic powder, brown sugar, and ginger. Just get it to a boil.

4. Lower the heat; cover the pot for twenty minutes. Just before eating, stir the lemon juice into the liquid.

5. In the liquid, prepare the veggies and protein and ladle pasta or grains over them.

Conclusion

Many Chinese are vegetarians because of the Buddhism faith i.e. adopting the Buddhist principles of less suffering. (less harm to the animals). Moreover, in China, many Yoga practitioners are vegans or vegetarians. To stay safe and active, Chinese people who are also not vegans or vegetarians choose to consume vegan dishes. In the same way as veganism is popular among people who have been very health-conscious in the West, Chinese also love to eat vegetarian food. Vegan diet and vegetarianism are still emerging as a movement in China. For older and more conservative persons, meat dishes are harmful to their health because of high carbohydrates and fats. This book has all types of vegetarian dishes categorizing into breakfast, snacks, lunch, dinner, soups, and some of the famous recipes of Chinese cuisine. Try these recipes and start preparing your easy and delicious vegetarian meals.